**DESIGNER'S
GUIDE TO**

SCANDINAVIAN

P A T T E R N S.

DESIGNER'S GUIDE TO

SCANDINAVIAN
P A T T E R N S

THOMAS
PARSONS

STUDIO EDITIONS
LONDON

First published in Great Britain in 1993
by Studio Editions Ltd
Princess House, 50 Eastcastle Street
London W1N 7AP

ISBN 1 85170 832 4

Printed and bound in Hong Kong

INTRODUCTION

Numbers in square brackets refer to plates and captions.

In Angus Wilson's novel, *Anglo-Saxon Attitudes*, Father Lavenham, an English clergyman, visits the Palazzo del Tè in Mantua, Italy, with an English professor of archaeology, Gerald Middleton, to look at the renowned sixteenth-century ceilings painted there by Giulio Romano:

'I hope,' said Father Lavenham, 'that I don't seem ostentatiously puritan, or rather, for once, I don't mind if I do, but I confess that all this Renaissance paganism is very antipathetic to me ... The vulgarity of Imperial Rome is unsavoury enough, this sort of imitation is unsufferable. It makes me glad that I am a medievalist ... But then I'm very English.

The history of Scandinavian pattern is interesting for much the same reasons as those that provoked Father Lavenham's rather quaint and decorous outburst. Not that many of the patterns illustrated in this book do not have their roots in paganism — for they do — but they speak of indigenous traditions and mythologies that lie resolutely outside mainstream European developments, centred as these are on Classical Rome and Renaissance Italy.

It is these shared traditions and roots that provide the fundamental link between the five countries of Scandinavia — Norway, Sweden, Denmark, Iceland and Finland, all of whose patterns will be brought together in this guide, and these, too, which seem to justify the grouping of these countries' patterns together in one book. And for these reasons, too, Finland is included as a Scandinavian country although linguistically and racially it is not.

As a result of the close connections linking these five countries, this introduction, as well as the layout of the plates that follow, has been organized along chrono-logical, not geographical lines. For, in any case, it was not until the Peace of Copenhagen, signed in 1660, that these countries' borders were settled more or less as they are today. Before that time, political relations between the five nations were unstable and closely, even confusingly, interlinked: Norway had been governed by both Denmark and Sweden; Iceland by Norway and Denmark; Sweden by Denmark and Finland by Sweden. This tangled and interlinked history justifies the grouping of these five countries together in this guide.

1 *These intricately carved, wooden mangle boards date from the seventeenth century and bear a pleasing mix of patterns, including a stylized dog, typical of the period. The boards were used for pressing handkerchiefs and other linen articles. They were carved with great skill as they were often given as pledges by men to their prospective wives.*

There are other reasons for the validity of speaking of specifically Scandinavian patterns. For one thing, each of these five countries came relatively late to Christianity. For another, they were each transformed, also relatively late, by the questionable benefits of industrialism. And for both these reasons, national and local traditions of craftsmanship and design continued to flourish and develop in an almost unbroken and uninterrupted line from ancient times.

2 *These gold brooches were uncovered as part of the Hornelund hoard in Denmark. The splendid filigree and granulation work indicate that these brooches were made for a chief or king. Viking men wore as much jewellery as the women – if not rather more.*

It remains a fact, however, that in the seventeenth and eighteenth centuries well-financed attempts were made in both Denmark and Sweden to establish viable, export-orientated silk and linen manufacturing industries **[70, 77]**. Immigrant weavers were encouraged to form part of the indigenous workforce. The textiles that were produced bore designs that followed patterns that were imported from France, Britain and Germany and were aimed at international markets. In both countries, however, the businesses floundered, while at the same time traditional, smaller crafts continued to be practised much as they had for hundreds of years. It is the patterns from these crafts that make up the bulk of the material illustrated in this guide.

Thus, for example, the motif of the horse in Norwegian ornament, first recorded on pre-Christian runestones, reappears in other media right up until the nineteenth century **[4, 33, 75, 78–84, 107, 108]**. The mysterious Runic script itself survived until the eleventh century, long after most other European countries had adopted the Roman alphabet. And in the seventeenth and eighteenth centuries, when Denmark and Sweden tried to encourage more modern manufacturing processes in the silk- and linen-weaving industries, native production was heavily protected by high tariffs from foreign imports. Even in the nineteenth century, wealthy farmers in southern Sweden commissioned costume ornament from local craftsmen that followed medieval patterns, spurning the more modern and fashionable imported patterns then available.

For reasons such as these, Scandinavian patterns display a peculiarly rigid conservatism. Folk traditions of ornament are, in any case, particularly resistant to change. Yet despite their conservatism, these patterns also testify to an extraordinary variety in their inventive and imaginative adaptation of stock forms and motifs.

One further reason needs to be mentioned to explain the unparalleled survival of so many ancient patterns from these countries – their geographical isolation. This is especially true of Iceland, the most inaccessible of Scandinavian countries and hence the most immune from stylistic developments going on in the rest of Europe. Colonized by Vikings at the end of the ninth century and converted to Christianity in 1000, Iceland functioned as an independent republic until 1262 when it ceded to Norwegian rule. In 1380, when the crowns of Norway and Denmark were united by marriage, Iceland became subject to Danish sovereignty. It regained its independence in 1944.

Throughout much of their history, Icelanders lived in rural communities, practising crafts such as weaving and woodcarving free from any urban or bourgeois patronage right up to the nineteenth century. The church naturally provided a focus for many of these local skills. Sadly, no medieval churches survive there today, and much of the pre-Reformation Icelandic wood carving was destroyed when the Roman church lost power **[45]**.

Nonetheless, the island's bleak, hilly

terrain supported large numbers of sheep. Their wool supplied cloth for the woven and embroidered textiles that became the mainstay of Icelandic folk craft tradition. If little survives today that predates the nineteenth century, it is clear that the patterns used on these colourful textiles were based on ancient and traditional models.

Iceland boasts little forested land. Wood is scarce. In rural areas, houses were, and still are, built of turf and heating is provided by burning peat. The wood that was used for domestic purposes tended therefore to be richly decorated, an indication of its rarity and value [1]. Moreover, to balance the expense of importing much of its wood, Iceland needed exports, and one of its principal sources of income came from preparing manuscripts. From the tenth century onwards, following the introduction of writing, brought to the country by the first Christian missionaries to travel to Iceland, copying and illuminating manuscripts developed into one of the country's largest industries. The importance of the written word is reflected in the patterns found on old wood carvings. Iceland, in fact, became the only Christian country to use lettering as ornament [67, 68].

The patterns and emblems that survive from the early tribal, agricultural communities of the other Scandinavian countries

3 This pattern shows one of the most ancient and enduring features of Scandinavian, especially Finnish, patterns – the giant and horses. The design probably has its roots in myth. It is tempting, for example, to attribute the giant who restrains the horses to Odin, the supreme, creator god of Scandinavian mythology.

display motifs such as the swastika and the solar disc common to many ancient cultures [7, 8, 9, 62, 86, 95]. Then, the eighth to the eleventh centuries saw the rise of the Vikings. During this period, the Scandinavian countries developed from loosely connected, predatory tribal structures into aggressive, organized states that at least professed allegiance to Christianity [37]. By the end of the period, however, it seems that the Vikings had become more concerned with profit than with war. Their ferocious, martial reputation was as much the product of later writers of the Nordic sagas as anything else. But, whatever the case, the period saw the change from communities that survived on subsistence farming into larger, national units wholly orientated towards trade. The Vikings, in their fast, shallow longships, travelled as far afield as Greenland, America, Ireland, France, England and Russia. Viking ornament was intended, by its ostentation, to be seen as a direct reflection of the Vikings' importance and trading prowess [2].

Geographical factors, as much as historical connections, have also played their part in the development of Scandinavian patterns. The lack of any large resources of gold or silver in the countries of Scandinavia stimulated the Vikings to steal or trade for it [12–15, 26–28, 33]. As a result, from a relatively early period alien styles of ornamentation began to influence native designs [29, 31, 36, 41–44, 50].

Denmark, like Iceland, lacks large areas of forest of its own and so most of its craft traditions have been built up in arts other than that of carving. The opposite is true of the densely forested areas of northern Norway, Sweden and Finland, where the tree appears as an integral part of many traditional patterns [4, 39, 47, 48, 78–87, 104, 107, 115–16]. It is also relevant to point out that some of the richest designs and patterns originated in the southern Scandinavian lands where the flat terrain and fertile soil brought wealth and power to the people who lived there. Again, however, the relative inaccessibility of large parts of each of these countries, with the exception of Denmark, has been a prime factor in the resistance to foreign influence characteristic of their patterns.

Foreign influences can, nonetheless, be discerned in the patterns that continued to be used in traditional crafts. These influences were, however, absorbed early on into the native tradition, such that while it is possible to see traces of Byzantine or Oriental workmanship in Viking or medieval Scandinavian patterns, these elements are invariably subordinated, never dominant **[25, 49, 57]**. Later, during the sixteenth and seventeenth centuries, when Danish and Swedish silks sought to emulate those being produced in France or Germany, it was the foreign stylistic influence that dominated.

Such early foreign influences on Scandinavian patterns can be detected as far back as the Viking age – the direct result of their extensive sea-borne trading activities. The Viking ships sailed both east and west. Viking merchants travelled down Russian rivers to make contact with the Eastern Empire, centred around the Black Sea. These merchants established trade routes with Byzantium where Nordic mercenaries are documented as serving in the Imperial Guard. They also founded colonies in Russia, as at Kiev, along the way. At Byzantium they could trade with Chinese and Syrian merchants. Viking remains have been excavated in modern-day Russia, while Byzantine, Chinese and Syrian remains have been found in Scandinavia. Indeed, Arabic, German and English silver coins dug up in their thousands at Viking burial sites testify to the volume of this trading activity.

These eastern connections proved highly influential in the development of Scandinavian patterns, influences which persisted long after the eleventh century when the trading links came to an abrupt halt with the Mongol invasion of Russia, which severed the economic connections between Scandinavia and the East. The

4 *The giant and horse motif was to undergo many changes, most significant of which was the metamorphosis of the giant into an enormous tree, possibly 'Yggdrasill' or tree of life. The horses here might also be seen as reindeer.*

lingering influence can be seen, for example, in the eastern-style 'onion' domes that crowned many Finnish churches built well into the seventeenth century. (Foreign influence can also be seen in the Italianate textile patterns that date from the fifteenth century **[51]**, but such patterns were invariably made for the artistocracy and upper classes and did not filter down into the craft tradition.) It was in this craft tradition, in the homespun textiles and lace embroidery, that the eastern influence had taken root, and it has survived up to the present century **[114, 120]**.

Most of the patterns illustrated in this book have sources in the social rituals of Scandinavian rural life: in other words, in the traditional crafts of embroidery, weaving, lace-making and wood carving. Thus, for example, the distinctive, brightly-coloured woven textiles made in the southern Swedish province of Skåne, from which a number of the patterns in this book have been taken, were produced for specific ceremonial occasions such as weddings, church visits and the like **[59–61, 66, 92, 98, 101]**.

Also, the recurrence, albeit highly abstracted and geometric, of the tree, the horse and the reindeer in many Norwegian and Finnish patterns has obvious roots in the fabric and routine of daily life in these countries' densely forested landscapes **[3, 40, 53, 98]**. Not only that, these motifs are symbols whose origins can also be traced back to old Norse mythology: to the 'Yggdrasill' or the tree of life, the roots of which reached down to the underworld while its top branches touched the heavens **[4, 46–48, 53, 75, 77, 78–84, 104, 107, 115–16]**; or to the 'bǎckahǎstar', sea or river horses that lured unwary humans into watery trouble **[8, 33, 58, 75]**.

These patterns then, were used to adorn textiles, vessels and the other artefacts of everyday life. They were produced for the family by the family. Until the seventeenth century, there was very little large-scale production of such articles; they were always part of much smaller, more intimate social units.

In 1910, a correspondent for a London magazine recorded this impression of Scandinavian rural life **[5]**.

... the everyday appearance of a Swedish peasant's home was chilling and still, but this appearance was altogether changed on the occasion of a festival ... when the walls and ceilings were covered with woven or painted hangings ... either of linen, woven, painted or embroidered, or else of paper on which figures were depicted. The woven cloths were adorned with geometric designs, or with patterns of severely conventional floral motifs ... amongst other things ... were gaily-coloured coverlets and cushions, the patterns of which show how highly developed the peasants' sense of colour was, and to what degree of excellence this home-weaving industry had reached.

Scandinavia did not, of course, remain totally closed to western European influences. As we have seen, pattern books from Germany, France and Italy began to disseminate quite widely during the sixteenth and seventeenth centuries. 'Yggdrasill' and 'bǎckahǎstar' however, proved strong enough to survive all the vagaries of imported foreign fashions.

5 *This photograph of the interior of a nineteenth-century Swedish log cabin gives some idea of the way in which locally produced decorative textiles were used in Scandinavia.*

6

Swastika

6 ■ The swastika emblem appears in the
centre of this pattern which has been
derived from a fifth-century picture stone
from Gotland, in Sweden. The Scandinavians believed the sign had magic prop-
erties and associated it with Odin who, as
well as being creator god, was also god of
magicians and seers.

7

8

12

9

Solar discs

7, 8 & 9 ■ These three solar discs, or sun symbols, have been taken from picture stones dating from the fifth and sixth centuries, found in Gotland. Each is surrounded by fabulous, mythical animals: coiled serpents **[7]**, flame-like horses **[8]** and reindeer **[9]**.

10

Reindeer

10 ■ Before the arrival of Christianity, Scandinavian nomads decorated the skins of their drums with symbols of their gods and animals of the hunt, such as these reindeer. Only a few of the drums survive as most were destroyed by the church. The writer Ernst Manker traced these designs from some of the few that survive.

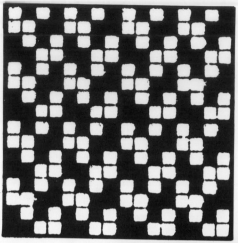

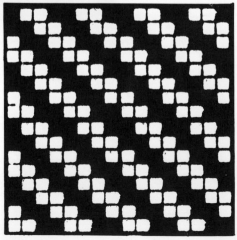

Weaves

11 ■ These five patterns have all been taken from ancient Scandinavian woven textiles dating from Viking and pre-Viking periods. The twill and dog's tooth patterns could date from Roman times. They have been found on fragments of clothing excavated in Norway and Denmark.

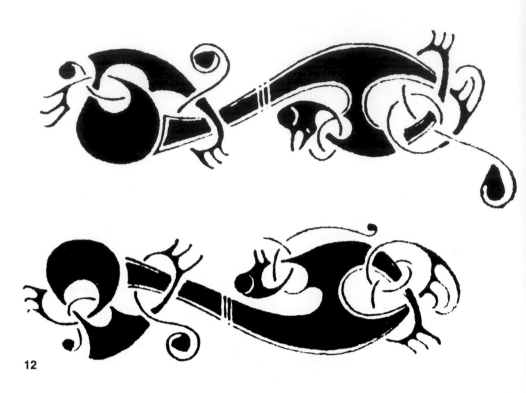

12

'Broa'

12 ■ This design and the following two are taken from a series of gilt-bronze bridle mounts found at Broa, in Gotland. They probably date from the late eighth or early ninth centuries and are among the earliest known Viking ornaments.

13 ■ More compact than the first, this animal motif is similarly sinuous with the body pierced at neck and hip. Tendrils are threaded through these openings. If the first motif seems serpentine, some of these second animal motifs are distinctly bird-like.

14 ■ This pattern is known as the 'gripping beast' – an immensely popular and widespread motif that is known of from the Broa find, but which persisted as the dominant motif in Scandinavian pattern until at least the eleventh century.

13

14

15

'Borre'

15 ■ 'Borre' is another early style of Viking ornament, dating from the ninth century. An interlace pattern is made up of a double ribbon arranged in rings and loops. This example has been taken from a gold pendant found in burial remains excavated at Hedeby, an important Viking trading centre in Denmark.

16

17

The Oseberg sledge

16 & 17 ■ These patterns are to be
found on the front and back of the body of
one of four eighth-century sledges found
with a Viking ship at Oseberg in Sweden.
Beneath a grid of geometric shapes lies a
barely distinguishable pattern of inter-
laced animals. These would have been
painted in red and black to make them
more noticeable.

18

The Academician's animal-head bed post

18 & 19 ■ Among the other artefacts discovered at the Oseberg ship burial mound were four sets of eighth- or ninth- century carved wooden bed posts, all based on animal heads. The posts were intricately decorated. The restless, inter- lace pattern is based on a bird motif.

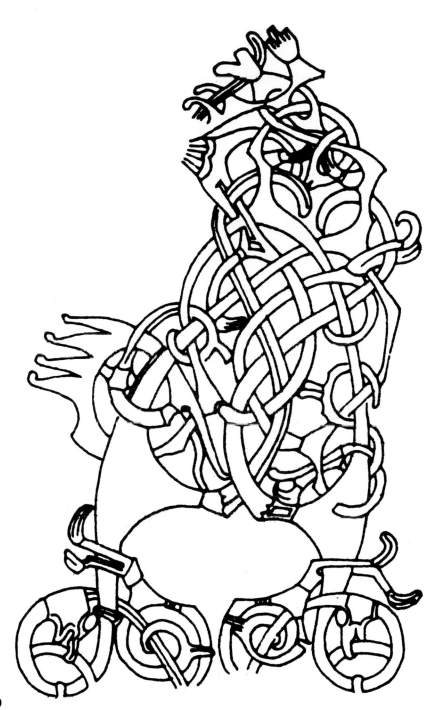

19

20

21

The Oseberg sledge

20 ■ This pattern is taken from the decoration on one of the poles from the Oseberg sledge **[16 & 17]**. As on the body of the sledge, the pattern here is built around a figure-of-eight animal body with a large dog's head.

The Baroque Master's second animal-head post

21 ■ Possibly slightly later than the Academician's bed post **[18 & 19]**, this pattern comes from one of the other wooden bed posts. Arranged within a framework of oval links, the carver here has based his pattern on the gripping beast motif **[14]**. But rather than depict whole animals, he has created his design using only disparate details – feet, tails, ribbons and flaps.

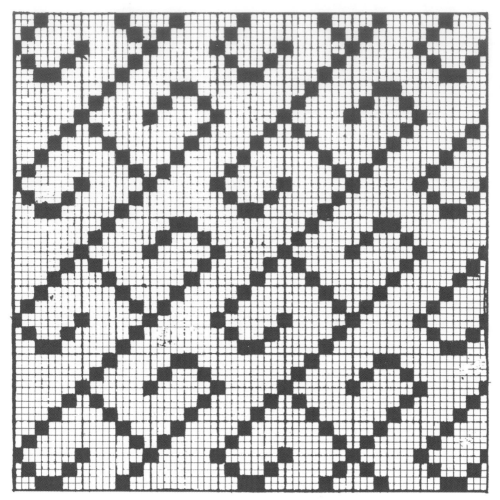

22

Horse

22 ■ This simple but elegant design comes from one of the earliest surviving Scandinavian textiles. Fragments of a large, pictorial weaving were discovered at the beginning of this century at a ship burial just outside Oslo, in Norway. They date from the middle of the ninth century.

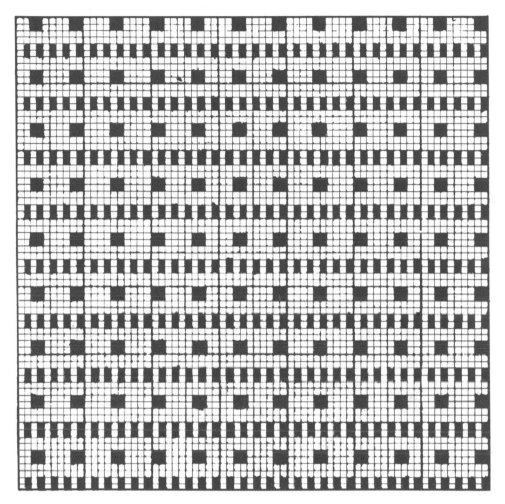

23

Check

23 ■ This banded, checkered pattern is also derived from woven fragments excavated at the Oseberg find. The burial mound was made for the Swedish Queen Åsa who died in the ninth century. This pattern was used on the leggings of a squire depicted in the textile.

24

25

Frieze

24 ■ Diamonds and crosses are combined in this more complex pattern, reconstructed by Sophie Krafft from the border or frieze of the Oseberg textile. All of the patterns derived from this source are highly geometric, but together seem to have been intended as a vivid testament to the variety of Viking textile design.

Key

25 ■ This elaborate pattern, dating from the ninth century, is also the work of Sophie Krafft [as are **22, 23** and **24**]. The pattern centres around a motif that seems directly related to the Greek key design. Though little survives today, textiles were evidently important to the Vikings. One of the later saga writers of the thirteenth and fourteenth centuries imaginatively recalls how, in the early twelfth century, King Sigurd of Norway stupefied the Emperor of Byzantium with the magnificence of his silk fabrics.

27

26

'Jellynge'

26 ■ Taking its name from a pattern that decorated a small silver cup found in a burial mound at Jellynge in Denmark, this is a slightly later style of Viking ornament that was used from the late ninth to the late tenth century. Its chief motif is that of a ribbon-shaped gripping beast. 'Jellynge'-style patterns are more graceful and elegant than their 'Borre' predecessors.

'Trewhiddle'

27 ■ This banded pattern is made up of alternate four-leafed plant and diamond forms. It has been taken from a double-edged sword pommel with silver plates, ornamented in 'Trewhiddle' style dating from the ninth century.

28

Asymmetry

28 ■ Viking craftsmen seem to have enjoyed creating patterns that suggest a
symmetrical arrangement but which, in
fact, end by confounding such expecta-
tions. This pattern has been taken from
part of a rectangular brooch, probably
from the tenth century, found in Denmark.

29

Ring

29 ■ The absence of any animal forms in these circular patterns of this tenth-century bronze buckle from Komnes, Sandsvaër, Buskerud is indicative of the influence of Celtic artists working in Ireland. Ring forms, however, were particularly widespread in Viking ornament but only rarely seen in Celtic art.

30

Cross

30 ■ This pattern derives from the carving of a stone cross that was found in the north of England. The animal and 'gripping beast' motifs, however, reveal that it must have been carved by a Viking craftsman for no animals appeared on Celtic crosses of the period.

Gaut

31 ■ Gaut was the name of a Norse stone carver working in the Viking-occupied Isle of Man in the tenth century. His work is distinguished by the integration of Celtic and Nordic motifs as in the split, plaited bands of this pattern that has been taken from a stone cross.

31

32

'Mammen'

32 ■ The name of this subsequent development in Viking tradition derives from a silver axe found in Mammen in Denmark. It seems to have grown directly out of the 'Jellynge' style **[see 26]**: the animal, however, is given more substance and, for the first time, is combined with curving plant-like tendrils.

'Ringerike'

33 ■ The 'Ringerike' style was prominent in the eleventh century. It elongates the 'Mammen'-style tendrils but also tends to subordinate plant forms to animal ones. The design has been taken from the gilded vane of a Viking longship; the beasts might represent the 'bảckahảstar' or horses of Nordic myth.

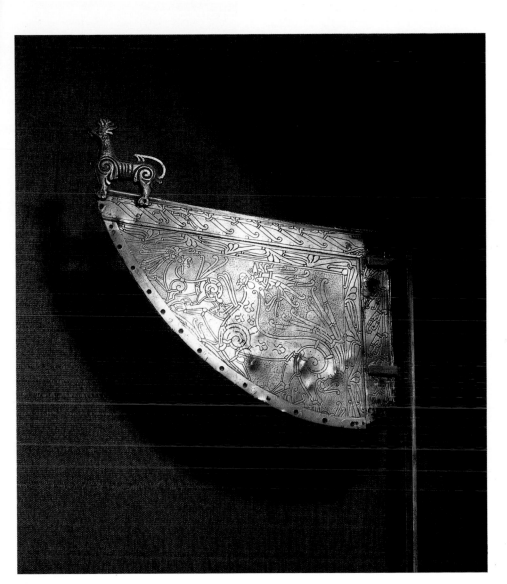

33

34

35

'Ringerike'

34 ■ The pattern is taken from a bronze panel, now in Winchester Cathedral, that was probably also originally part of a ship's gilded vane. Above the centre, one of the main branches terminates as an animal head. At the corresponding point below, both of the branches are being eaten by a small snake.

'Urnes'

35 ■ The 'Urnes' style represents the final, most delicate and refined flowering of Viking ornament. It was extant only during the eleventh century. The name drives from the carved, wooden decoration of a church in the town of Urnes in western Norway, from which this pattern has been adapted.

36

'Urnes'

36 ■ This example of 'Urnes' style has been taken from a late eleventh-century gravestone from Gotland in Sweden. Thereafter, the independence of Viking ornament began to decline. During the twelfth century, while the Scandinavian nations drew closer to the rest of Europe, their patterns began to show the influence of Romanesque styles.

37

The Skog Church wall hanging

37 ■ The majority of Scandinavian medieval textiles have not survived. Many must have been destroyed – first when the advent of Christianity rendered pagan subjects undesirable, and second when ecclesiastical subjects were deemed blasphemous during the Reformation. This detail is from one of the few that has survived, found in a church in Hälsingland, Sweden. The three figures to the right are ringing bells to frighten off evil spirits and pagan gods, an indication of the tension that existed for many years between old religion and new. It has been dated by historians as having been made between 1050 and 1200.

38

The Kungsåra bench

38 ■ This early twelfth-century bench from Kungsåra Church in Sweden was probably carved for a local lord or prince. Only the back, which would have faced the rest of the congregation, has been decorated.

The Rogslösa Church door

39 ■ A hunting scene fills the top section of this twelfth-century door from the church at Rogslösa in Sweden. Beneath it is a compressed version of the Fall, Redemption and Last Judgement. The decoration is made of fluted and incised sections of wrought iron strapwork that have been riveted onto the wood.

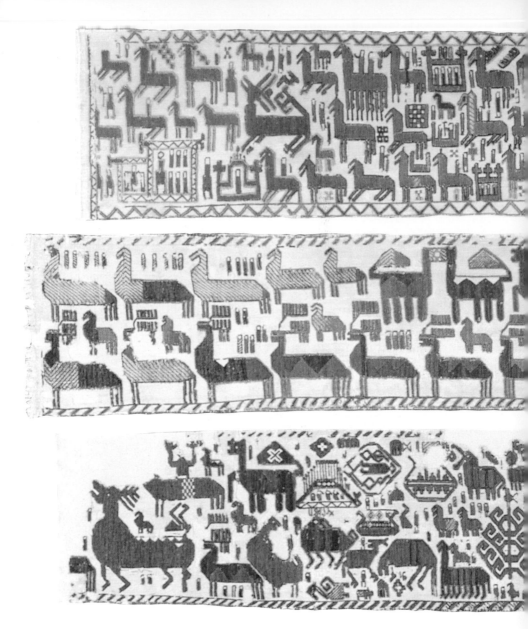

40

The Överhogdal tapestry

40 ■ The familiar beasts of Scandinavian mythology inhabit this Swedish double-weave tapestry that dates from the Middle Ages and comes from Härjedalen in Sweden. Reindeer, crested birds, horses and riders surround the stylized motif of the 'Yggdrasill'. These ancient subjects were soon replaced by Christian ones.

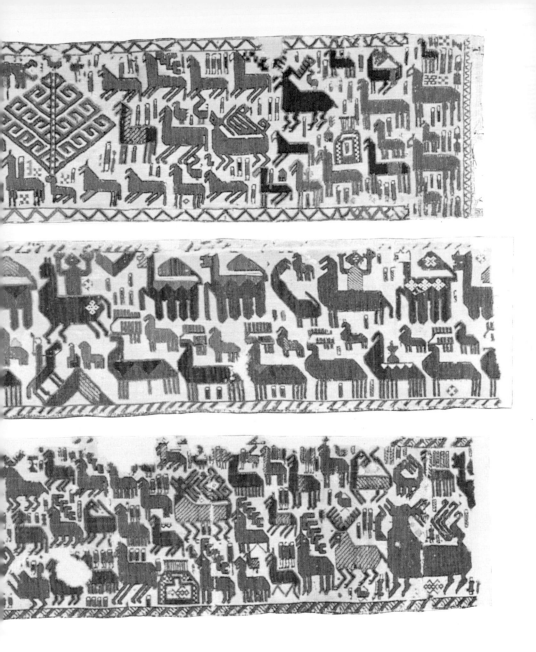

41

The Baldishol tapestry

41 ■ This fragment from a twelfth-century Norwegian tapestry was discovered in a church at Baldishol in the nineteenth century. The whole piece depicted the different months of the year.

The two figures that survive represent April and May. The wave motif in the upper border, as well as the acanthus leaf motif in the lower, reveal the influence of Romanesque designs.

47

42

43

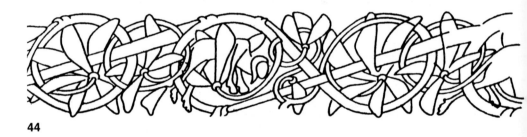

44

Three church roof beams

42, 43 & 44 ■ The roof beams of ancient Scandinavian churches, even the most humble, were often carved and painted in rich colours. These three, from churches in Sweden, were probably made in the twelfth century. The first **[42]** uses a flowing, interlace design originating from Viking ornament. The other two **[43 & 44]** include more complex floral and animal motifs – an indication of Scandinavian craftsmen's fascination with the new Romanesque and Byzantine patterns which were becoming increasingly popular throughout Europe.

45

Lions

45 ■ Two lions, heraldic symbols of power, are set into square frameworks, their bodies and heads intertwined with ornamental tendrils. The pattern was carved in pine onto the door of a wooden cabinet found in Iceland. It probably dates from medieval times.

46

47

48

Horses and giants

46 ■ Two riderless horses face each other in mirrored poses in this medieval border pattern derived from embroidered clothing from the Karelia region in Finland. In between them, the traditional figure of the giant stands with arms raised. The motif, however, threatens to lose itself within an increasingly geometric schema.

Horse and tree

47 & 48 ■ The same motif lies behind each of these traditional, medieval Finnish patterns for embroidered border bands – a central tree flanked by two horses. When, however, the bands were widened and the pattern repeated in reverse beneath, their roots in myth and legend became difficult to recognize. Nonetheless, such roots probably lie behind this widespread and peculiarly Scandinavian predilection for geometric patterns.

49

50

Key
49 ■ Taken from a fragment of a Danish medieval textile, possibly part of a woman's headdress, this pattern could be described as an elaborate variant on the traditional Greek key design. Trade connections between Scandinavian countries and the eastern world make such an influence distinctly possible.

Romanesque
50 ■ This pattern is derived from the chancel decoration of an early medieval church in Jutland. Following the end of the Viking era, around the eleventh century, decorative procedures in Scandinavia began to adopt, albeit a little unsubtly, the Romanesque patterns that were widespread throughout the rest of Europe.

51

The golden gown

51 ■ This evidently Italianate pattern has been taken from the wedding dress of the fourteenth-century Swedish monarch, Queen Margaretas. The central motif of a pomegranate, the symbol of fertility, was a graphic invocation for a blessed union.

Quatrefoil

52 ■ Two light quatrefoil frames form the dominant motif in this pattern from a mid-fifteenth-century altar fabric from Herrestad Church, in Gotland. The emergence of such a typically Gothic motif indicates a growing awareness among the Scandinavians of European developments, for example such as that fostered by Saint Birgitta in the late middle ages. She founded an influential textile school at the convent in Vadstena in Sweden.

52

53

The Nådenals Abbey Church wall hanging

53 ■ Familiar motifs from Scandinavian mythology fill this watercolour showing a detail of sixteenth-century (Finnish) wall hanging: the crested birds, reindeer and the Yggdrasill. The central octagonal panels probably tell the story from some folktale or heroic saga.

54

55

The wise and foolish virgins

54 ■ Dating from the Reformation, this cushion was probably made to celebrate a marriage. Both virgins and suitors sport sixteenth-century collars in a conscious effort to make the Biblical parable contemporary. Traditional pre-Reformation patterns, however, fill the border.

Gothic

55 ■ Gothic patterns travelled as far north as Finland by at least the early sixteenth century. In this pattern from a panel of an ecclesiastical embroidery, made for the church in Kiir Kala, large flowers lie within the flowing, scrolled stems of a framing medallion. Branched leaflets fill the corners. Each panel seems to have been made up of fragments of old clothing that were sewn together before being embroidered with gilt membrane.

56

The North-Voguls saddle pad

56 ■ This pattern, probably from the six-teenth century, uses negative repetition, a common device where patterns were stitched onto woven supports and hung from the walls of a church or a house. The technique was popular because it saved precious material.

57

Evangelists

57 ■ Fabulous beaked birds and bearded lion-like beasts, each armed with jagged claws, alternate in bands in this design from a medieval Finnish church embroidery, probably sixteenth century. They could represent the traditional symbols of two of the evangelists – John (the eagle) and Mark (the lion). Another school of thought holds that they are heraldic animals, an important influence from Finland's earlier trading connections with Byzantium.

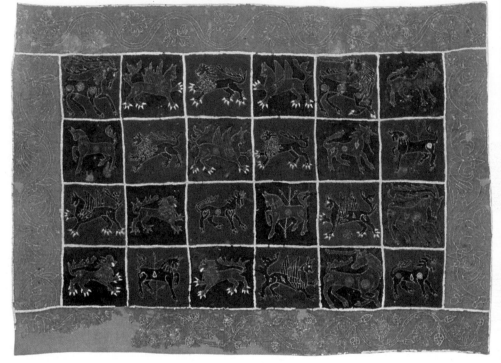

58

Negative

58 ■ Horses, dragons and reindeer, doubled and reversed in the manner of the image and its photographic negative fill the squares of this pattern. It has been taken from a sixteenth-century church hanging from Skepptuna in northern Sweden. It is extraordinary how long such ancient motifs as these continued to be used in ecclesiastic decoration.

59

Bridal double-weave

59 ■ The bride with her crown, in the left-hand corner, leads a procession of riders in this fragment of a seventeenth-century double-weave textile from Kyr-kejebø in Norway. These articles were specially woven for the marriage cere-mony and would have been part of a bride's trousseau.

60

61

'Riddarateppid' (Coverlet of Knights)

60 ■ Each of the panels of this seventeenth-century Icelandic bed cover seems to relate to an episode of some lost saga or epic. The whole cover was woven in long-arm cross-stitch. Scenes of the hunt had magical associations for many Icelanders, with characters being led in and out of different adventures.

Eight-point star

61 ■ A design for a chair, carriage or sleigh cushion, executed in long-arm cross-stitch, probably during the seventeenth century. This technique produced heavy, tapestry-like textiles which were very strong and durable. They almost always used geometric patterns. The eight-point star was one of the most widely used motifs of this time.

63

Solar discs

62 ■ Solar discs are an ancient motif found in many different cultures all over the world. These three variations are each derived from woodcarvings from a seventeenth-century Swedish church.

Arabesque

63 ■ The delicately executed forms of this floral motif have been taken from a seventeenth-century Danish silk embroidered tablecloth. The arabesque pattern has probably been adapted from a French original or modified from an imported pattern book.

62

64

'Maaling'

64 ■ Examples of 'Maaling' decoration, brightly-coloured patterns painted on domestic wooden furniture, originated in Norway at least as early as the late Middle Ages. These patterns were also painted onto wooden walls of domestic interiors. By the seventeenth century, from which time this pattern dates, floral or fruit-based motifs tended to have displaced the geometric frames of earlier examples. The predilection for plant-based 'Maaling' was probably stimulated by contemporary, imported European fabrics.

Bound Rose-Path

65 ■ Rose motifs were particularly popular in Norway and Sweden and can be found in textile patterns which date from medieval times. This pattern, probably from the seventeenth century, would have been either embroidered or woven onto the borders of tapestries or the sleeves of shirts, blouses and jackets.

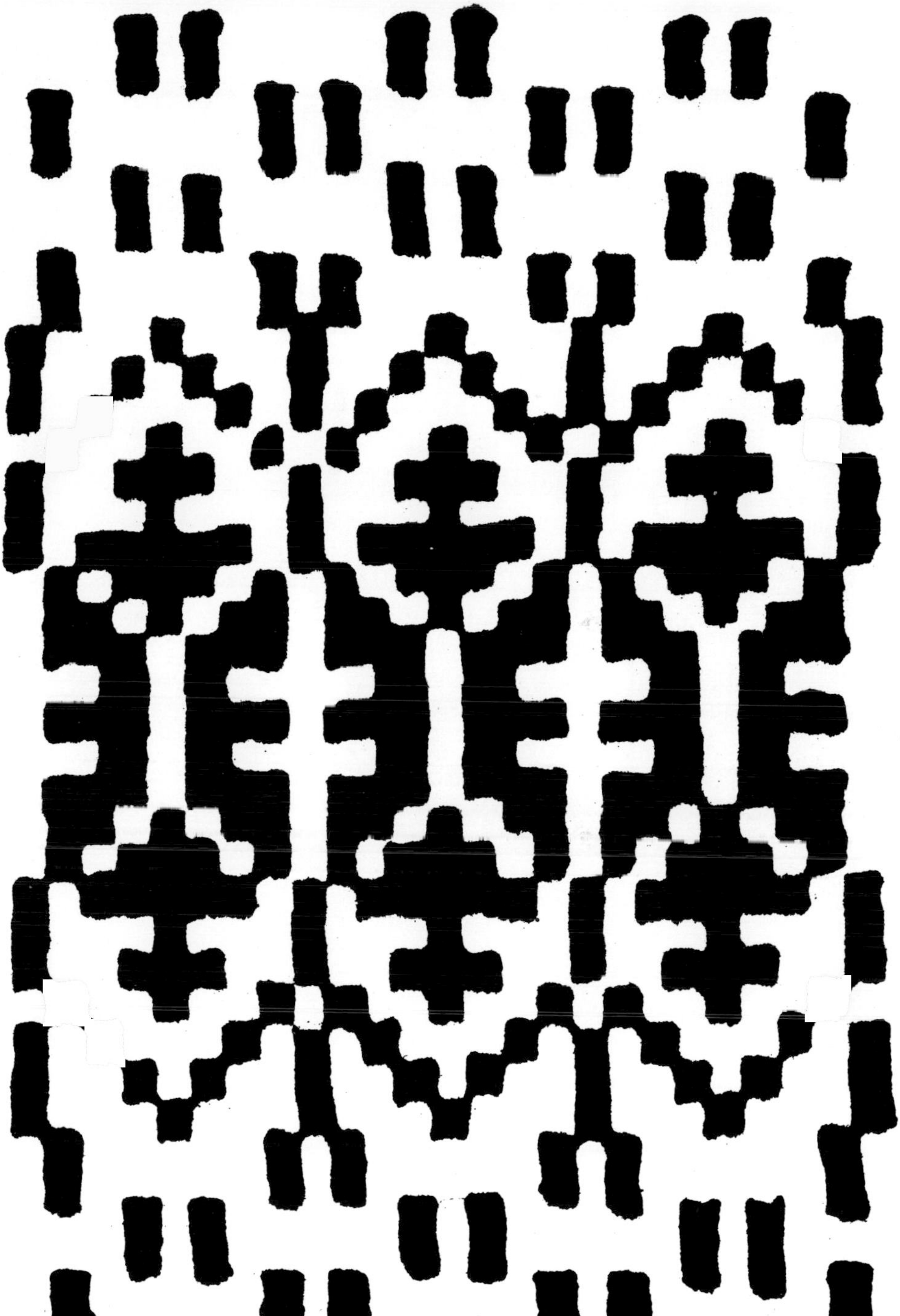

65

66

'Rölakan'

66 ■ A 'Rölakan' was a type of double-sided, interlocked tapestry that was produced in the rich plains of southern Sweden. The tapestries, hung on the walls of peasants' and farmers' dwellings on special occasions, were highly coloured and also displayed predominantly floral and geometric patterns.

Calligraphy

67 ■ Taken from a seventeenth-century mangle board of carved pine, this pattern has cleverly manipulated the letters of an inscription into an ornate, decorative format. Icelandic craftsmen were unique in western Europe for creating patterns out of the abstract graphic potential of letters of the alphabet.

Tendrils

68 ■ Gracefully carved tendrils from a seventeenth-century Icelandic mangle board curl and intertwine. The crisp detail and flowing rhythms testify to that island's strong native tradition in manuscript calligraphy that dates from the tenth century.

67   **68**

69

70

Annunciation

69 ■ This Scandinavian tapestry, which probably dates from the early eighteenth century, depicts an Annunciation scene. The angel points to a bird in a tree, possibly a pelican or heron, both of which had traditional symbolic associations with Christ's sacrifice and victory over death.

Rya

70 ■ Ryas are thick, double-pile rugs that date back at least as far as the tenth century AD. Initially they were plain, but by the late eighteenth century Swedish women had begun to decorate them with designs from imported pattern books. This is based on French and German models.

71

72

Geometry

71 ■ Many Scandinavian patterns are geometric, not only because these shapes and forms suited these people's expressive needs, but also for technical reasons. Woven textiles, for example, were made on looms on which it was not possible to create curved or organic shapes. This pattern is taken from a fragment of an eighteenth-century Icelandic woven bedspread.

'Maaling'

72 ■ This panel from a trunk made in 1776 is a fine example of a 'Maaling' pattern favouring curved tendrils or plant-based forms that seem to be distantly related to earlier forms of decoration [see **45, 50, 68**]. Their eventual root would seem to lie in the Scandinavian countries' absorption of the Romanesque.

73

Figured double weaving

73 ■ This pattern, with its stylized bird, leaf and female figure motifs, is characteristic of peasant variations of figured double weaving in 'tabby' binding. It dates from a Swedish counterpane woven in Bohuslän, around 1787, by a farmer's wife probably during the winter when days were short and nights long.

74

Coffin cloth

74 ■ This highly intricate and richly col-oured wool embroidery, woven in Norway in 1796, was made as a cloth to be laid on a coffin – to play a part in the social ceremony of funeral and mourning. The inclusion of so many different motifs lends the cloth an unexpected celebratory rather than a lugubrious note.

75

Bench cushion

75 ■ This pattern is taken from a twentieth-century copy of an original nineteenth-century Danish bench cushion. The original would, itself, have been based on older examples. The horse, one of the most ancient motifs in Scandinavian patterns, reappears here amid giant blooming flowers.

Rya

76 ■ This Finnish rya rug, made in 1820, is remarkable for the simplicity and highly abstracted nature of its design. Its stark geometry and bright colour both seem to anticipate many more modern patterns.

76

77

Baroque

77 ■ Two crested birds face each other in this design taken from an early nineteenth-century Danish embroidery.

They are surrounded by a panoply of blooms and tendrils. These motifs are traditionally Scandinavian. However, they

have been naturalistically described – an indication of Baroque French or German influence prevalent at the time.

78

Horse and tree

78 & 79 ■ The familiar motifs of horse
and tree were adapted for the square
format of the embroidered chests of two
traditional blouses from the Tchouvache
district of Finland in the nineteenth century. Here, double-headed horses, each
sharing one rider, are separated by the
diagonal accents of the tree. Extreme
thematic limitations evidently fostered the
widest variety of decorative patterns.

79

80

Horse and tree

80 & 81 ■ These two squared patterns, also adapted from nineteenth-century Finnish blouses from Tchouvache, use the tree motif as the main diagonal form. The horses seem momentarily to have disappeared. For all their variety, however, the women who invented these patterns never departed from their ancestors' commitment to the geometric and abstract.

81

82

Horse and tree

82 & 83 ■ Faint vestiges of the tree and
horse are discernible in these two Finnish
patterns, again taken from the embroidered chest pieces on nineteenth-century
blouses. We shall never know for sure
whether or not the women who designed
these patterns were aware of their roots in
ancient myth.

83

84

85

86

Amalgam

84 ■ An amalgam of favourite mythic Finnish motifs has been arranged around an equal-sided, bordered cross. They include horse and rider, cockerels and crowned love birds. The pattern again derives from a nineteenth-century embroidered blouse. The central female figure might possibly represent Freyja, the goddess of plenty and prosperity.

Horse and tree

85 & 86 ■ The double or mirrored horse, as well as the tree, appears again in the Finnish patterns used here on the embroidered borders of peasant blouses, from which this design is taken. The design also incorporates the ancient swastika motif [see **6**], traditionally associated with magical invocations for the blessing of the Scandinavian gods.

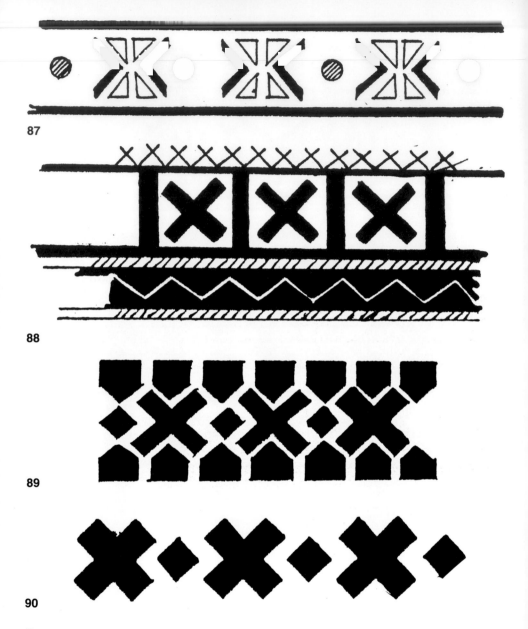

87

88

89

90

Cross

87, 88, 89 & 90 ■ These variations on a basic cross motif have been taken from nineteenth-century Finnish folk embroidery. They would have been used on the borders, sleeves and seams of homespun garments. The Finnish craft tradition, and this distinguishes it from the other Scandinavian countries, has always enjoyed decoration for its own sake, perhaps by virtue of its extremely close contacts with its powerful neighbour Russia and eastern ornamental influences.

91

Star

91 ■ Tendrils and abstracted flower motifs fill this star pattern. Star shapes on dark backgrounds were particularly popular in Iceland, and this design is based on a nineteenth-century Icelandic bedspread. Such textiles would often provide the only touch of colour within the spartan interior of the house.

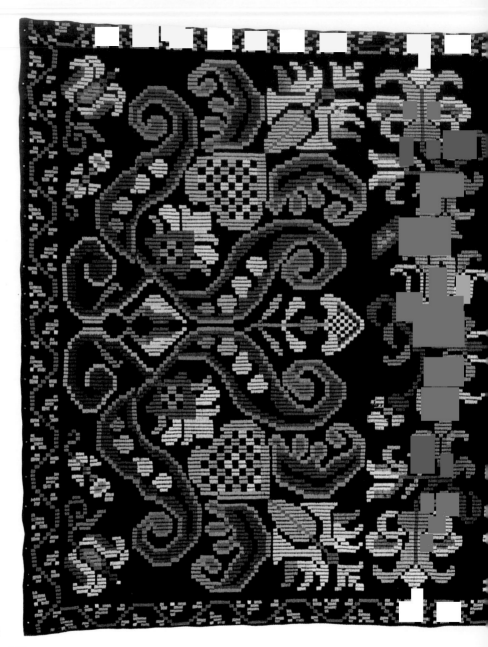

92

Saddle cover

92 ■ This pattern has translated the organic curves of a floral motif into geometric terms. It has been taken from a nineteenth-century Icelandic woven cloth saddle cover, and would probably only have been used on specific ceremonial occasions, such as weddings or especially important church visits.

93

94

96

95

96

Revival

03, 04, 05, 06 & 07 ■ These five patterns are amongst many traditional woven and embroidered designs from Finland that were collected and published in the late nineteenth century. The first **[93]** is obviously floral in inspiration, but unusual in that it eschews the geometric treatment so integral to Finnish patterns. The second and third **[94, 95]** both use the swastika motif as a point of departure. The swastika, despite its present associations, traditionally symbolized an invocation for the blessing of the gods and can also be found on Viking burial inscriptions. The fourth **[96]** derives from embroidered borders, a design with a simple, basic form

97

manipulated to produce a subtle and intricate pattern. The fifth **[97]** is a Finnish variant on the widespread Swedish 'Vigg' or lightning pattern.

98

Landscape

98 ■ Sun and moon shine down, side by side, on the endless ranks of pine trees beneath a horizon of mountain peaks in this design taken from a Finnish 'Tåkånå' tapestry. It would have been boldly coloured and hung on special occasions in the home.

Diamond

99 ■ Diamond lozenges variously arranged in clusters on a monochrome background, and aligned in horizontal bands separated by stripes, is a pattern found on rugs and tapestries throughout Finland. The colours would have been made from natural dyes.

Tree

100 ■ This old pattern is taken from a nineteenth-century Finnish woven tapestry. A bold, lone and drastically stylized pine tree forms the central motif, surrounded by an angular interlace design. Mirrored patterns such as these were known as 'Moskve', an indication of the Finns' close contacts with Russia.

101

Eight-point star

101 ■ Traditionally Scandinavian brides would make and embroider large, billowing shirts for their husbands. These would be decorated on collar, cuff and front placket. This eight-point star pattern is taken from a cross-stitched band from Telemark in Norway.

103

'Lokki' (Gull)

102 ■ The sinuous curves of Art Nouveau inform the rhythms of this early twentieth-century Finnish rya rug designed by Jarl Eklund. However, the muted colour scheme of black, brown and white looks back to previous ages before wool was dyed.

'Lisko' (Lizard)

103 ■ Designed by Finnish textile artist Aksel Gallen-Kallela in 1904, this rya rug depicts a scene from the *Kalevala*, a national epic poem. On the banks of the River of Death sits a lizard, its long tail nestling amongst sharp and bloody rocks.

104

Nursery
104 ■ This twentieth-century pattern, a somewhat simplistic, representational and alternate design of reindeer and trees, derives from a 1930s adaptation of a traditional Danish nursery hanging. It stems originally from an eighteenth-century pattern book.

Stocking
105 ■ This pattern, again adapted from traditional sources in the 1930s, is taken from the fragmentary border of what seems to be an eighteenth-century stocking found in a remote fishing village in Jutland, Denmark.

Shawl
106 ■ In the past, Danish mourning shawls, though sober in colour, did include small areas of decorative embroidery. In the Reformation, however, such frivolity was banished and the shawls became purely black. Old patterns, such as this one, were later resuscitated, as for example in this 1930s design.

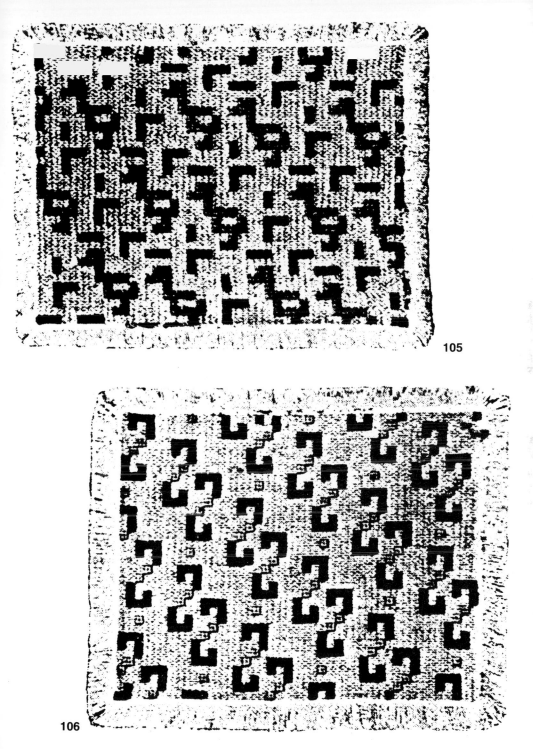

105

106

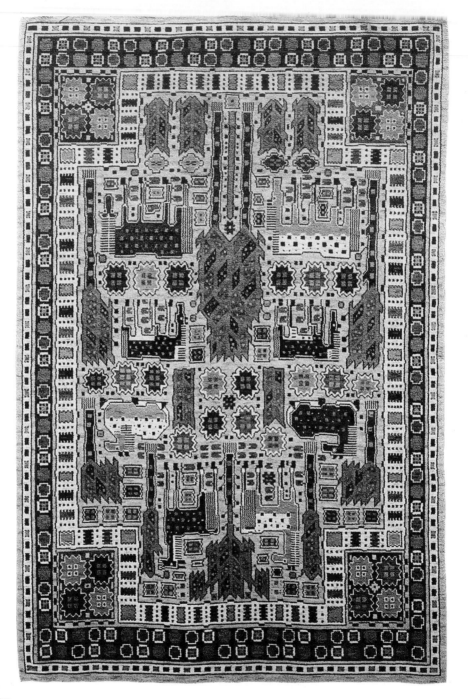

107

108

Horse and tree

107■ Until her death in 1941, Märta Måås-Fjetterström was one of the most influential of a number of pioneering twentieth-century Swedish weavers. She sought to keep alive traditional weaving techniques and designs, such as the horse and tree motif seen in this pattern, which as we have seen, is one of the most enduring of Scandinavian patterns.

'Lozenge twill'

108 ■ This woollen rug was made in Sweden in the late 1920s. The pattern has been described as 'lozenge twill' and has been found on fragments of textiles that date from pre-Viking times.

109

Vine

109 ■ This simple vine pattern was designed by the Finnish textile design Eva-Stina Dahlqvist in the early 1930s. It was produced for fine damask fabrics used for domestic purposes. Despite the Bacchanalian theme, the design is characterized by its elegance and austerity.

110

Needlethread

110 ■ This Finnish needlethread pattern was embroidered onto a simple, striped woollen bedspread, made in 1932. The pattern was never used commercially, but provides another example of the way in which traditional handcrafted designs with centuries-old origins have survived into the present century.

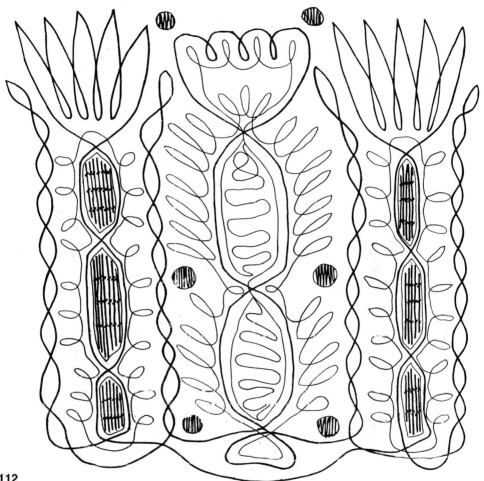

112

Frieze

111 ■ This Swedish 'rölakan', or double-weave rug was woven during the 1930s. It would have been produced in the home. The pattern has survived more or less unchanged since Viking times **[see 24]**.

Stem and Flower

112 ■ Within a square format, stand three, highly-stylized plant forms, each crowned with a flower. Stem and flower alike are linked by two separate but mirrored threads of interlace in this modern adaptation of a traditional, Finnish embroidered pattern.

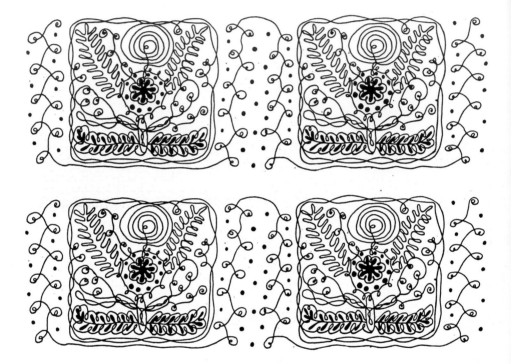

113

Flowers and leaves

113 ■ Not all Scandinavian patterns, even the most ancient, are geometric. In this 1950s adaptation of a traditional border motif from a Finnish woven tapestry, a nervous line freely describes flowers and leaves within a loose square framework. Each square is surrounded by an equally spindly interlace pattern.

114

Finnish traditional

114 ■ It is not certain, in this 1950s adaptation of an old Finnish motif traditionally embroidered on cushions and rugs, whether the form has roots in the human or animal world. Its similarity to certain traditional Swedish patterns suggests common sources in Oriental or perhaps Byzantine textiles.

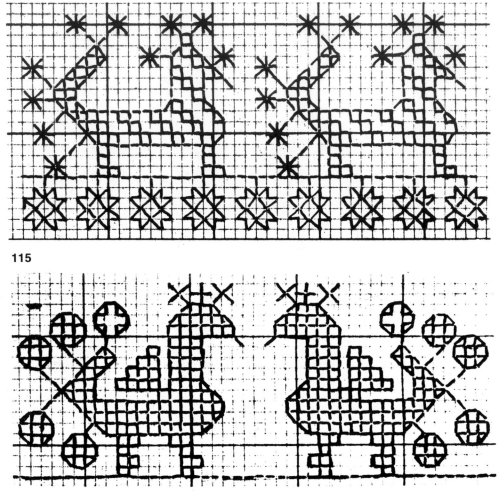

115

116

117

Birds

115 & 116 ■ In these two patterns, adapted from the 1950s from an old Finnish lacework, the ubiquitous crested bird makes another appearance. In Nordic mythology, a cockerel was said to perch at the top of the 'Ygddrasill' to warn the gods of the approach of the belligerent race of giants.

117 ■ Mirrored pairs of birds with outstretched wings share a diamond shaped head. Each pair is separated by a ten-branched star. This pattern has been taken from a design made in the 1950s, but it is based on traditional Finnish lacework which was commonly used for shawls and table linen.

118

Marimekko: 'Trakatori' and 'Villinarsissi'

118 & 119 ■ One of the most influential textile-producing companies, Marimekko from Finland, was founded in the 1960s. The patterns its designers have invented are characterized by their boldly simpli-fied lines and sweeping organic rhythms, as can be seen in these two silk-screen cotton prints by Maija Isola. Marimekko designs, both for their textiles and for clothing, enjoyed widespread internation-al success throughout the 1960s and 70s.

119

120

Jette Valeur Gemzøe

120 ■ This woven carpet was made and designed by Danish textile artist Jette Valeur Gemzøe. She has taught in Copenhagen and Canada and runs her own workshop in Turkey, a contemporary counterpart to the traditionally strong links between Scandinavian patterns and eastern decorative arts.

119

121

122

Vigg
121 ■ This is a modern 'rya' rug whose pattern is based on one of the most popular and oldest Scandinavian patterns, the 'Vigg' or lightning design [see **98**]. Rya rugs were traditionally often given as presents by prospective husbands to their fiancées.

'Hvid vinkel'
122 ■ This woven carpet was made by Danish textile artist Jette Kastberg. The title translates as 'White Angle'. Her work, like that of her compatriot Jette Kai, [see **123**] aspires to the world of fine arts rather than that of applied or decorative arts.

123

Jette Kai

123 ■ The Danish textile artist Jette Kai designed and made this woollen carpet. She has transposed the predilection for the geometric Scandinavian patterns found on embroidered or woven clothing to an article destined as much for the museum as for the home.

Violet

124 ■ Dora Jung was an influential Finnish fabric designer who turned her attention to traditional woven damasks in the 1950s and 1960s. These had normally always been either of pure white or, subsequently, decorated with a narrow and repetitive stock of floral motifs. This detail is from a pattern designed for table linen and reveals how, under the influence of oriental design, Jung was able to revitalize an old tradition. Designs such as this paved the way for further innovations in Finnish fabric design in the 1970s.

124

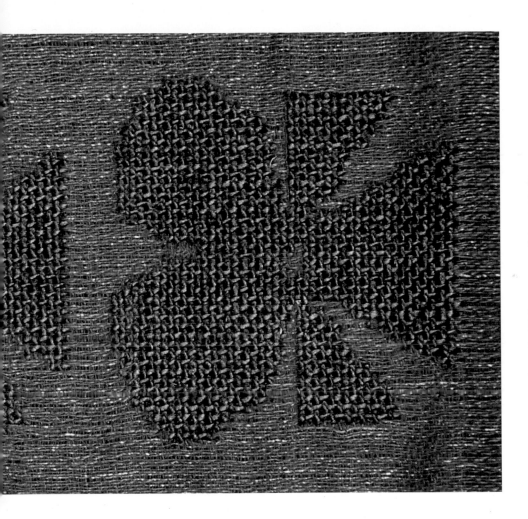

125

'Harlekiini'

125 ■ The Swedish designer Marjatta Metsovaara based this design for a printed cotton sateen on the traditional diamond pattern of the Harlequin's cos-tume. She has deliberately disrupted the normally regular geometry of the pattern – a modification common to many Scandinavian textile designs that were produced in the 1960s and 1970s.

BIBLIOGRAPHY

Anker, Peter. and Andersson, Aron *The Art of Scandinavia*, 2 vols, London, New York, Sydney, Toronto, 1970.

Beer, Eileene Harrison. *Scandinavian Design: Objects of a Life Style*, New York, 1975.

Black, D., Willborg, P. and Loveless, C. *Flatweaves from Fjord and Forest*, London, 1984.

Eldjárn, K. *Icelandic Art*, London, 1961.

Foote, P.M., and Wilson, D.M. *The Viking Achievement*, London, 1970.

Graham-Campbell, J. and Kidd, D. *The Vikings*, London, 1980.

Grimal, P. (ed.) *Larousse World Mythology*, London, 1965.

Hald, M. *Ancient Danish Textiles From Bog and Burial*, translated by J. Olsen, Copenhagen, 1980.

Krafft, S. *Pictorial Weavings from the Viking Age: Drawings and Patterns from the Oseberg Finds*, Oslo, 1956.

Martin, E. and Sydhoff, B. *Swedish Textile Art*, translated by W. Barrett, Stockholm, 1979.

Nodermann, M. *Nordic Folk Art*, Stockholm, 1988.

Olki, M. *The Handicrafts of Finnish Women*, Helsinki, 1952.

Paine, S. *Embroidered Textiles: Traditional Patterns from Five Continents*, London, 1990.

Pylkkänen, R. *The Use and Traditions of Medieval Rugs and Coverlets in Finland*, Helsinki, 1974.

Riiff Finseth, C. *Scandinavian Folk Patterns for Counted Thread Embroidery*, Seattle, 1987.

Shetelig, H. *Viking Antiquities in Great Britain and Ireland*, 6 vols, London, 1940–1954.

——— 'The Norse Style of Ornamentation in the Viking Settlements', *Acta Archaeologica*, 19, (1948), 69–113.

Skovgaard, I.W. *The Technique of Tønder Lace*, London, 1991.

PICTURE ACKNOWLEDGEMENTS

Photo ATA, Stockholm 6. Joseph Anderson *Scotland in Pagan Times: The Iron Age*, Edinburgh, 1883 27. Peter Anker and Aron Andersson *L'Art Scandinave*, Zodiaque, Ste Marie de la Pierre qui Vire, St Léger Vauban, 1969, 16, 17, 18, 19, 20, 21, 42, 43, 44. Archäologisches Landesmuseum der Christian-Albrechts-Universität, Schleswig 15. David Black Oriental Carpets, London 69, 76. Brages Samlingar, Helsinki/photo Bertil Bonns 1932, Svenska Litteratursällskapet i Finland, Folkkultursarkivet 110. The Embroiderers' Guild Collection/photo Julia Hedgecoe 75. P.M. Foote and D.M. Wilson *The Viking Achievement*, Sidgwick and Jackson, London, 1970 12, 13, 14, 30. photo Föreningen Svensk Form, Stockholm 107. Fylkesmuseet for Telemark og Grenland, Skien/photo R.A. Haugen 64. Agnes Geijer *A History of Textile Art*, Pasold Research Fund in Association with Sotheby Parke Bernet, London, 1979 65, 66. Jette Gemzøe 120. J. Graham-Campbell and D. Kidd *The Vikings*, British Museum, London 1980 32. Jämtlands Läns Museum, Östersund 40. Lise Bender Jorgensen *Forhistoriske Textiler i Scandinavien*, Det Kongelige Nordiske Oldskriftselskab, Copenhagen, 1986 11. Jette Kai 123, Laila Karttunen *Kirjontamalleja*, Werner Söderström Osakeyhtiö, Helsinki, 1950 100, 112, 113, 114. Jette Kastberg 122. Sofie Krafft *Pictorial Weavings from the Viking Age: Drawings and Patterns from the Oseberg Finds*, Grøndahl Dreyer, Oslo, 1956 22, 23, 24, 25. Kunstindustrimuseet, Oslo/photo Bridgeman Art Library, London 41. *Kvadratsting Danske Originalmønstre: Samlet og Udgivet af Clara Wæver*, Copenhagen, 1933 104, 105, 106. André Leroi-Gourhan *Documents pour l'Art Comparé de l'Eurasie Septentrionale*, Les Éditions d'Art et d'Histoire, Paris, 1943 3, 4, 46, 47, 48, 78, 79, 80, 81, 82, 83, 84, 85, 86, 87, 88, 89, 90. M. Mackeprang *Jydske Granitportaler*, Høst & Søns Forlag, Copenhagen, 1948 50. Marimekko Oy, Helsinki 118, 119. Marthas Textilarkiv, Åbo/photo Arne Appelgren 1928, Svenska Litteratursällskapet i Finland, Folkkultursarkivet, Helsinki 108. Marthas Textilarkiv, Åbo/photo Hjördis Dahl 1931, Svenska Littertursällskapet i Finland, Folkkultursarkivet, Helsinki 109. Museo Virasto, Helsinki 53, 55, 56, 57, 98, 99. Nationalmuseet, Copenhagen 28, 49, 63, 77. Nationalmuseet, Copenhagen/photo Werner Forman Archive, London 2. Nordiska Museet, Stockholm 10, 61, 70, 73, 91. Nordiska Museets Arkiv, Stockholm 5. Norsk Folkemuseum, Oslo 54, 59, 72, 101. Norsk Folkemuseum, Oslo/photo Bridgeman Art Library, London 74. Mary Olki *The Handicrafts of Finnish Women*, Werner Söderström Osakeyhtiö, Helsinki, 1952 115, 116, 117. Axel Poignant Archive, London 7, 8. Private Collection, Korpo (Houtskär)/photo Maj-Gun Åberg 1974, Svenska Litteratursällskapet i Finland, Folkkultursarkivet, Helsinki 111. Private Collection, Lappträsk/ photo Mirja Vasama 1982, Svenska Litteratursällskapet in Finland, Folkkultursarkivet, Helsinki 121. *Proceedings of the Society of Antiquaries of London*, 2nd series, 23, 1911 34. Rogslöca Church/photo Zodiaque, St Léger Vauban 39. P.T. Schvindt Suomalasia Koristeita: Finnische Ornamente 1, Helsinki, 1895, 93, 94, 95, 96, 97. H. Shetelig (ed) *Viking Antiquities in Great Britain and Ireland*, 6, Oslo, 1954 31. Statens Historiska Museum, Stockholm 52, 58. Statens Historika Museum, Stockholm/photo ATA 36. Statens Historiska Museum, Stockholm/photo Werner Forman Archive, London 9, 37. Statens Historiska Museum, Stockholm/photo Zodiaque, St Léger Vauban 38. Taideteollisuusmuseo, Helsinki 102, 103, 124, 125. Thjødminjasafn Islands, Reykjavik 1, 45, 60, 67, 68, 71, 92. Uno Ullberg, Alarik Tavaststjerna, Jalmari Kekkonen *Kansanomaisia Rakennustapoja ja Koristemuotoja Karjalasta*, Helsinki, 1929 62. Universitetets Oldsaksamling, Oslo 26, 29. Universitetets Oldsaksamling, Oslo/photo Werner Forman Archive, London 33. Uppsala Cathedral/photo ATA 51. Urnes Stave Church/photo Werner Forman Archive, London 35.